If people are proud and unreasonable, misguided and selfish,
Love them anyway.

If you are kind, and people say that you do it for selfish reasons,
Be kind anyway.

If you succeed, but find only untrue friends and true enemies,
Succeed anyway.

If the good deeds you do today are forgotten tomorrow,
Do good deeds anyway.

If being truthful and saying what you believe hurt you,
Tell the truth anyway.

If things you spent years building are destroyed overnight,
Build anyway.

If you help those in need from the goodness of your heart,
and they attack you,

Help anyway.

If you give the world the best you have, and you are kicked
in the teeth,

Give the world the best you have anyway.

—Mother Teresa

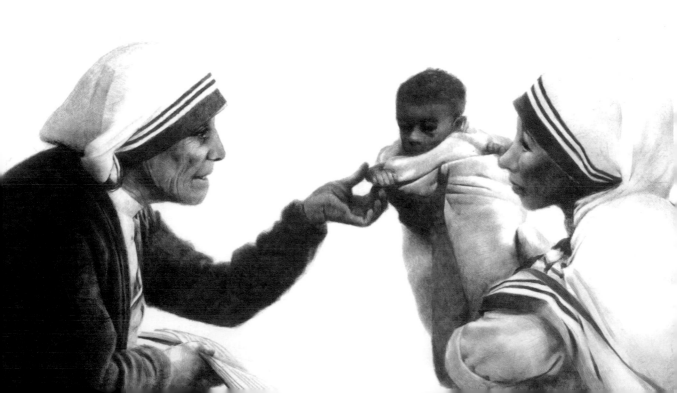

Mason Crest
450 Parkway Drive, Suite D
Broomall, PA 19008
www.masoncrest.com

Printed and bound in the United States of America.

First printing
9 8 7 6 5 4 3 2 1

Series ISBN: 978-1-4222-2839-5
ISBN: 978-1-4222-2853-1
ebook ISBN: 978-1-4222-8973-0

Cataloging-in-Publication Data on file with the Library of Congress.

Produced by Vestal Creative Services.
www.vestalcreative.com
Illustrations copyright © 2000 Robert Ingpen.

People of Importance

MOTHER TERESA: Religious Humanitarian

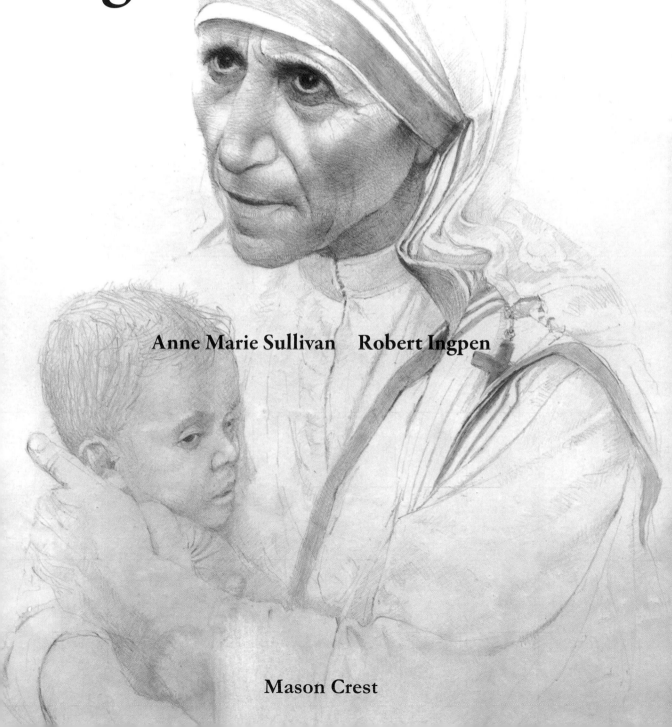

Anne Marie Sullivan   Robert Ingpen

Mason Crest

Today I am taking a very big step. It is the most important decision of my life. I am going to become a nun. I am joining the Order of the Missionaries of Charity. Once I take my vows today, I cannot change my mind.

My family is Catholic. They understand why I want to become a nun, but they wonder why I chose this order. They are worried about me. They know I face a future filled with very hard work. Most people cannot even imagine it. "Are you sure?" they ask me. "Have you truly thought about it?" "I chose this order because of Mother Teresa," I tell them. "I want to be like her."

I still remember the first time I met Mother Teresa. She was tiny, thin and bent with age and hard work. Her face was spiderwebbed with fine wrinkles, and her hands looked like tree branches covered with blue veins. Her blue and white habit had seen many washings. It had faded and dulled with time.

To me, she was beautiful, and I felt drawn to her like a magnet to metal. Kindness, tenderness and holiness shone from her like sunlight. Her eyes seemed to look deep inside me, and they were filled with love and concern. From her tightly pressed mouth, I could tell that she would never quit when she had a job to do. I felt as if I had known and loved her all my life.

In many ways, she reminded me of Jesus' mother, the Blessed Virgin Mary. Like the Virgin Mary, Mother Teresa loved all God's creatures. On her thin shoulders, she carried the problems and sufferings of all the world's poor people.

Looking at her, I could see the starving, the sick, the homeless and the lonely people she loved and served every day. Her wrinkles, her bent back, her worn hands and her faded clothes were signs of her work. They made her look more beautiful and more holy. I knew then that I wanted to follow in her footsteps and join the order of nuns that she started.

I sit here reading the Bible, getting my mind, heart and soul ready for the life I begin today. Many years ago, Mother Teresa took her vows as a nun. She was a young woman like me. I try to imagine her on that day. I wonder—did she feel the way I'm feeling right now?

When Mother Teresa was born on 26 August, 1910, her parents named her Agnes Gonxha Bojaxhiu. Her parents came from Albania, but she was born in the city of Skopje. Today Skopje is in Macedonia, a country near Greece.

There were three children in her family, and she was the youngest. Agnes's father was a builder and a businessman. Her mother was very religious. She worked hard to take care of her children and to bring them up as good Catholics. Agnes had a happy and comfortable childhood until her father died suddenly. After that, her mother was left to raise the family by herself.

Life was hard for the family then, and they didn't have much money. But there were strangers at the family supper table nearly every day. When Agnes asked who they were, her mother always told her, "They are our relatives." They weren't really, but Agnes knew her mother's heart must be filled with love. She took in people she didn't know and treated them like her own family. From her mother, Agnes learned a lesson that stayed with her when she decided to spend her life serving the poor.

When she became a teenager, Agnes liked to spend time at church. She joined a youth group that helped the priests, nuns and other members of the parish. Here, an idea came to her. She thought about travelling to far-off countries to do God's work. One of her parish priests told her to listen to God's voice speaking inside her. He said that if she felt great happiness in her heart, she would know she was making the right decision. She felt deep down that she was being called to tell the whole world about God.

Deciding to leave her home and family was not easy for Agnes. Her mother helped her, explaining that her job in life would be special. She would be able to give her whole life to others, taking the church as her home and all people as her family. Not everyone had the chance to live so selflessly. Her mother's love and support helped Agnes to feel that she was making the right choice.

Many years later, Mother Teresa said, "I am Albanian by birth. Now I am a citizen of India. I am also a Catholic nun. In my work, I belong to the whole world. But in my heart, I belong to Christ." That was Mother Teresa. She was a mother to the world. Her heart belonged to God, while she used her body to help the suffering every day.

Agnes travelled to Ireland to join the Sisters of Loreto convent in 1928. She was 18 years old. In Ireland, she studied to become a nun and learned English. People there remembered how kind she was and how hard she worked to learn English.

For a long time, Agnes had been hearing God's voice inside her. The voice told her, "Go to India and serve it." Her wish came true on 6 January, 1929, when she arrived in India. Her first job there was to teach religion and geography at St. Mary's High School in the city of Calcutta. She also went to school herself. She was still studying to become a nun. She worked some more on her English and began learning two Indian languages, Hindi and Bengali.

Life in the convent was hard. There was not enough food to go around. Each nun received a small, carefully measured amount every day. The nuns

also did heavy work. The hot, damp weather was very different from the climate in Europe where Agnes had grown up. These strains on Agnes's body made her sick. She might have had tuberculosis, a disease that makes breathing difficult.

She had to leave Calcutta for a while. After she got better, Agnes returned to Calcutta and went back to her work. She took her final vows and became a nun in 1931. She took the name Sister Teresa. Her life in the convent was quiet and peaceful. The nuns lived behind high walls and followed strict rules that told them how to live.

But outside the convent walls, India was in trouble. The streets of Calcutta were filled with starving beggars. People had to drink from the sewers. On her walk between the convent and St. Mary's school, Sister Teresa met Calcutta's poor. She noticed how they were suffering

The whole world was caught up in World War II. Many in India had to leave their homes.

Some of them came to stay at St. Mary's Loreto Convent, where Sister Teresa lived. By living side by side with these people, she saw their daily lives and their suffering in a new way. War outside changed life inside St. Mary's too. There came a time when Sister Teresa's students had nothing to eat. The streets outside were filled with fighting and danger, but Sister Teresa went out to search for food.

Outside, she found burned buildings. She saw wounded people crying in pain and dead bodies lying in the streets. In the middle of this confusion, Sister Teresa searched for a way to help her hungry students. Suddenly a truckload of soldiers stopped in front of her. "Get back to your convent!" the officer in charge shouted.

Sister Teresa did not even stop to think before speaking. "I have 300 students who have no food. If I can't find food for them, I will not go back." The soldiers looked at this tiny nun standing so bravely in front of them. She looked as if she herself hadn't eaten in a few days. The soldiers wanted to help her. They searched for food and gave her some of their grain. Then they drove the food to the school in their truck. In these soldiers, Sister Teresa saw God helping her, and she thanked him. She knew that she would not have been able to save her students from starving without his help.

Sister Teresa loved teaching and her life in the convent. But she had witnessed so much suffering during her time in India. She had much to think about. In 1946, when she was 36 years old, Sister Teresa heard God's voice deep inside her once again. God told her, "Go to the poorest of the poor and serve them." As always, Sister Teresa listened to God's voice.

Sister Teresa asked the bishop in Calcutta to let her leave the convent and live in the slums. He did not think this was a good idea at first. He was worried. The bishop wondered, would Sister Teresa stay healthy and safe living with the poor? But Sister Teresa kept trying, and two years later, in 1948, the bishop gave his permission.

On 16 August, Sister Teresa said goodbye to her students. The girls loved their principal, and they would miss her. Many of them cried as they lined up in front of the convent.

Sister Teresa's body was not big and strong. But her love and her faith in God were so strong that nothing could stop her. After leaving St. Mary's Loreto Convent, she learned how to nurse the sick at the Holy Family Hospital. She learned how to feed patients, give shots and deliver babies.

The sick people she helped loved her for her patience and kindness. They could feel her love for them. The work was very hard, and Sister Teresa was exhausted, but she never complained. She was always ready to care for her patients.

In the beginning, Sister Teresa worked alone. She didn't talk about her work or ask anyone for help. But some of the girls she taught at St. Mary's came to help her.

Together they worked and struggled against many things that stood in their way. In time, they became a new order of nuns, the Missionaries of Charity. On 7 October, 1950, Pope Pius XII gave the new order his blessing.

Now Sister Teresa was Mother Teresa, the leader of a community of sisters who help the poorest of the poor. With these nuns at her side, Mother Teresa found more ways to comfort the poor and sick. She felt that very sick people who have no homes should have the chance to die with peace and respect. So they wouldn't have to die in the streets, she started a home for the dying called the Nirmil Hriday.

You must understand the poor
Before you can love them.
You must love them
Before you can serve them.

(Mother Teresa wrote these words in 1971.)

Mother Teresa also took care of people with leprosy. Many people were too afraid of this disease to touch people who suffered with it. For children with no parents, she started an orphanage. Now these children could grow up in a home with people to care for them.

Mother Teresa taught her sisters to rely on prayer for strength as she did. She once said, "We do hard work. Prayer can support us, help us and enable us to accomplish what we must do joyously." We begin every day with prayer, getting out of bed at 4:30 every morning to prepare for matins, our morning prayers, at 5:00.

Our life in the convent is very simple, with no luxuries. I can easily count everything that I own on my fingers. Each sister has only two habits, one to wear while the other is being washed. One pair of sandals and two pairs of stockings are our only other clothing. We each have one iron plate for meals, a cotton quilt and a bucket. We wear coarse underwear that doesn't soften until it has been washed at least ten times. On the outside, our life appears to be hard and uncomfortable. But inside, our spirits are calm, peaceful and filled with joy. We know we have God's work to do.

The older nuns tell me the work was much tougher when Mother Teresa was alive. It was prayer that kept her going. She said, "Had it not been for praying, I would not have been able to sustain half an hour of work. Only through praying can we get strength from Our Lord."

While I was training to become a Missionary of Charity, I worked as an intern nun. I spent two or three days each week helping the nuns with their work. Sometimes we walked the streets passing out food to hungry people. Other times, we visited the sick in hospitals or very old people.

Mother Teresa loved children, including those who were still waiting to be born. "The unborn infants are the poorest among the poor. They are nearest to our Lord," she said. She wanted all children to be loved and wanted by their families. She also believed that all people, born and unborn, have a right to live and be cared for.

Although she no longer taught school full time, Mother Teresa still felt that education was the key to a better life for all children. With knowledge, people have choices; they don't have to be poor.

Mother Teresa dreamed of an education for all children. She passed this dream on to her nuns. Although they had no money for a building and school supplies, the nuns created a makeshift blackboard by clearing the grass from a patch of dirt. They taught poor children by writing in the dirt with sticks. With no desks, no chairs, no chalk and no pencils, these children learned to read and write.

Over time, that patch of dirt grew into a school. Inspired by Mother Teresa, people began making donations. One would give tables and chairs. Another might have classroom space to give. Mother Teresa eventually founded more than 140 schools in India. But she never wanted any of them to be named for her.

Her love for poor children also drove Mother Teresa to establish orphanages to care for children with no parents.

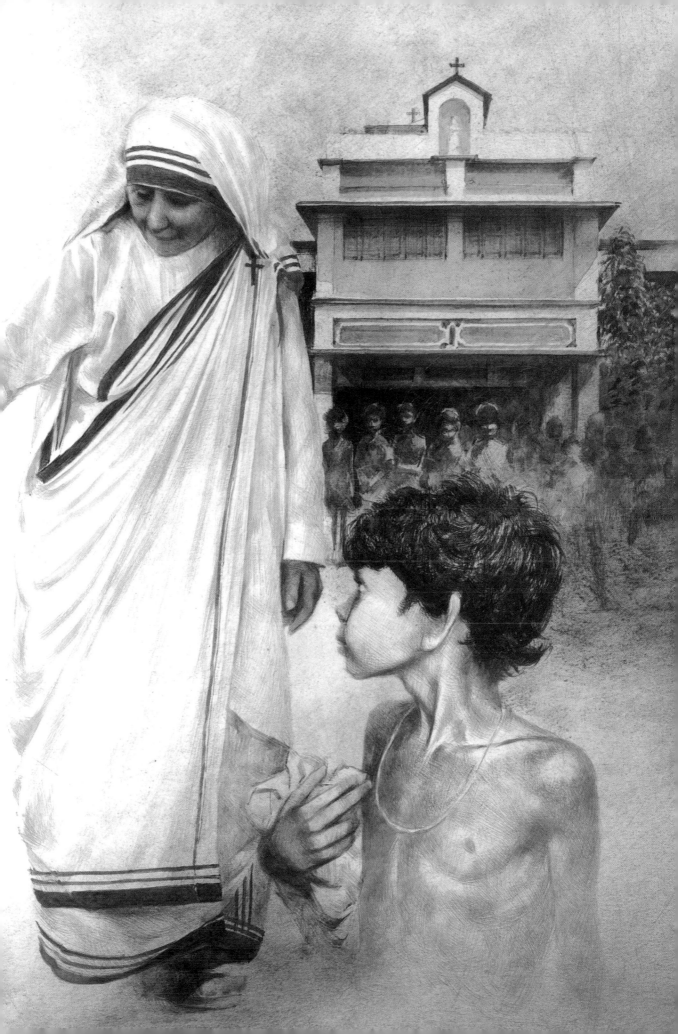

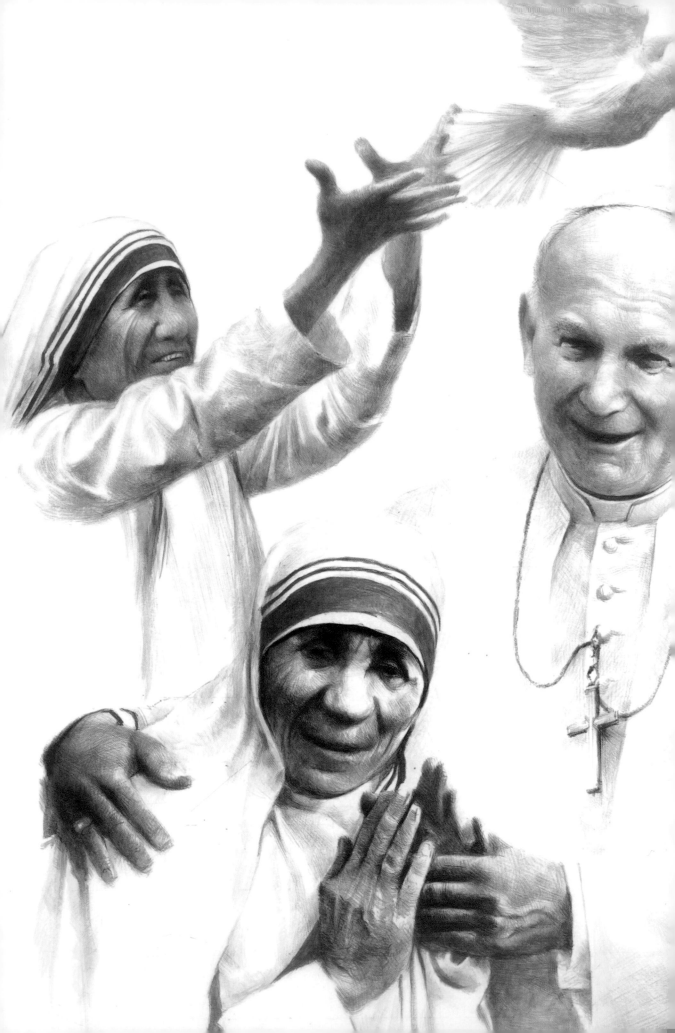

On 11 December, 1979, Mother Teresa was awarded the Nobel Peace Prize, one of the greatest honours the world has to offer. The ceremony took place in Oslo, the capital of Norway. Many famous and important people from all over the world were present. Most were dressed in their richest, finest clothes.

During the ceremony, Mother Teresa entered wearing her usual faded blue and white habit. She stood in front of all those famous people and spoke to them. Her speech was slow and her manner calm, as if she were talking with her close friends. She reminded her audience that there are poor and sick people all over the world who need help.

Unlike the other women there, she wore no makeup or jewelry. She didn't even change into a new habit for this special occasion. But she stood out among these gorgeously dressed people as the most beautiful person in the room. She was radiant that day as the love in her heart shone for all to see. That special day, like every other day, she cared most about the poor and the sick. Helping them was what truly mattered to her.

Mother Teresa met many famous people during her lifetime. She was very close to Pope John Paul II, the leader of the Roman Catholic Church. But she was never awed by wealth or fame.

She died on 5 September, 1997. At first, those of us she left behind felt lost without her. Who would encourage us and give us strength when we felt weak, we wondered. Who would comfort us when we felt sad? Who would help us when we didn't know what to do? Could we continue this work without her guidance?

She is gone, but the poor and sick are still all around us. Their soiled bed sheets still need to be washed. Their sores and wounds still need to be dressed. They still need to be fed and cared for. We looked around us and knew we had to keep working despite our deep sadness.

Sometimes I feel better when I remind myself that Mother Teresa's body was too tired to go on anymore. God invited her to put down her worldly cares and join him in heaven. At last, she can rest.

At our convent, we pray every day for God's strength as Mother Teresa taught us to do. We pray to the Virgin Mary to bless us with peace and courage. And we pray to Mother Teresa in heaven to help us now as she did when she was alive.

Today, there are Missionaries of Charity working in more than 70 countries around the world. In a different way, Mother Teresa is still leading us. She brought the world's attention to the needs of the poor. Many people admired her and want to help us in our work. We receive money, letters and prayers from all over the world. With this help, we can keep working, spreading love to every corner of the earth.

If people are proud and unreasonable, misguided and selfish,
Love them anyway.

If you are kind, and people say that you do it for selfish reasons,
Be kind anyway.

If you succeed, but find only untrue friends and true enemies,
Succeed anyway.

BIOGRAPHIES

Author Anne Marie Sullivan received her Bachelor of Arts degree in English from Temple University. She has worked in the publishing field as a writer and editor. She lives with her husband and three children in the Philadelphia suburbs.

Illustrator Robert Ingpen was born in 1936 in Geelong, Australia. Ingpen's earliest work was the sketch of a shell he did when he was young. His first job, at the age of 22, was to draw illustrations and design publicity pamphlets for CSIRO, a scientific research institution. All of his illustrations were related to various scientific research reports. The work honed his perception and established his realistic style of painting. Interestingly, Ingpen's illustrations sometimes inspired scientists to explore and study the subject at hand from new perspectives. This is where the charm of Ingpen lies.